CONTENTS

FOREWORD

Whenever indicated (next to tempo marking in each piece), all eighth notes in that composition should be played as "jazz triplets" to achieve a more authentic jazz sound.

Example: ♩ ♩ ♩ ♩ played as ♩ ♪ ♩ ♪
(long short long short)

It should be emphasized to students that triplet (long-short) interpretation of 8th notes is a *jazz* phenomenon only, and is not employed in other musical idioms such as classical or even rock music.

The composer strongly urges the pianist to strictly observe all interpretive marks (staccatos, phrases, etc.) in this volume.

The composer gratefully acknowledges the editorial assistance provided by Marcia Klebanow for this book.

Music Engraved by Irwin Rabinowitz

EXCLUSIVELY DISTRIBUTED BY

Piano Plus, Inc. | Hal•Leonard CORPORATION

7777 W. BLUEMOUND RD. P.O. BOX 13819 MILWAUKEE, WI 53213

Jazz It Up!

LEE EVANS

* See Foreword regarding "*jazz triplet*" interpretation of eighth notes.

Example: (Bar 1) | (long) (short) (long) (short) | played as | ... |

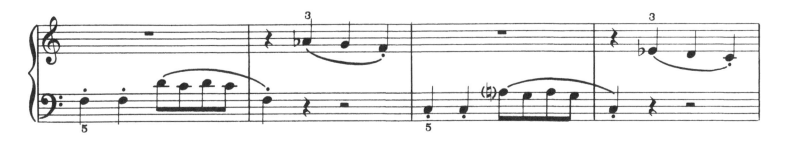

Jazzmatazz

LEE EVANS

Cheerfully, with a bounce (♩ = 92)

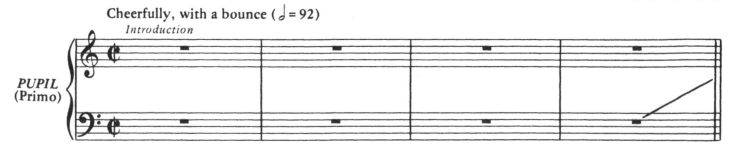

Cheerfully, with a bounce (♩ = 92)

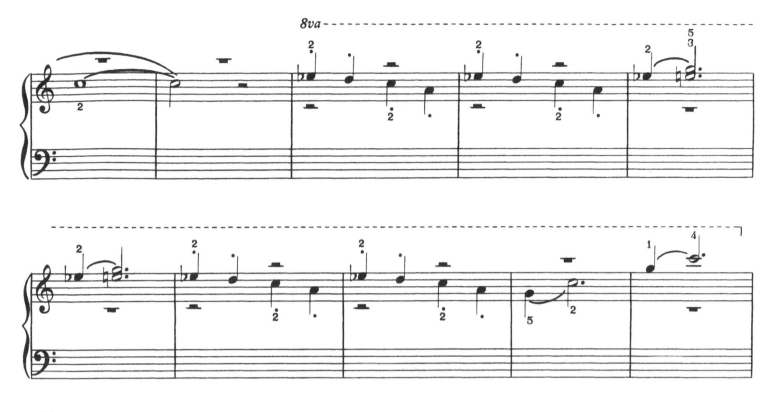

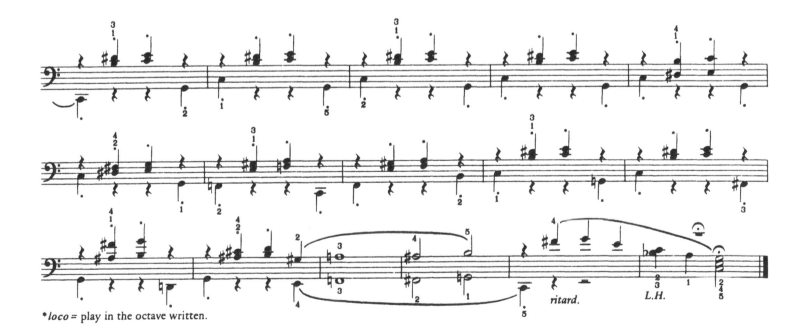

*loco = play in the octave written.

Cool Dude

LEE EVANS

In swing style (♩ = 144)

PUPIL
(Primo)

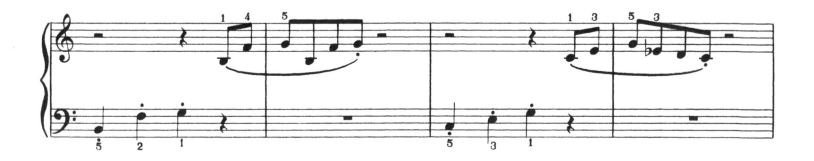

TEACHER
(Secondo)

In swing style (♩ = 144)

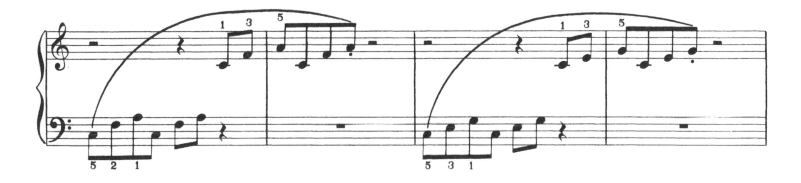

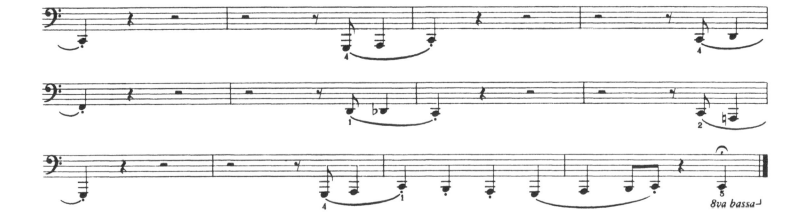

PP-3

Boogie Woogie

LEE EVANS

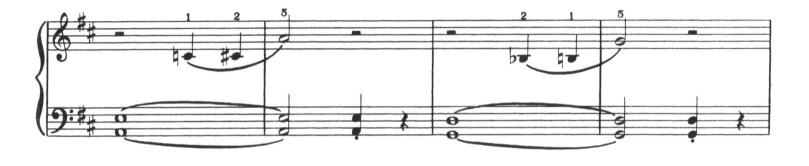

PP-3

Loco Motive

LEE EVANS

Big Tease

LEE EVANS

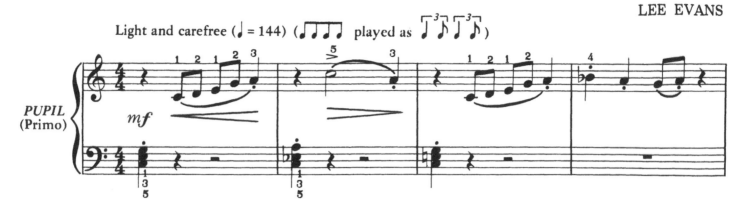

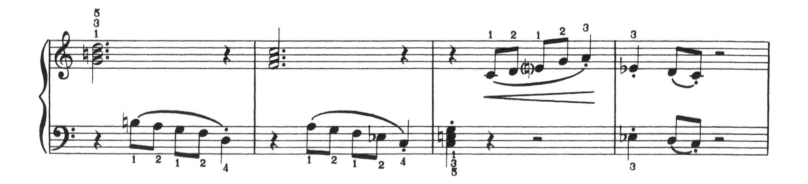

Bach To Trinidad

LEE EVANS

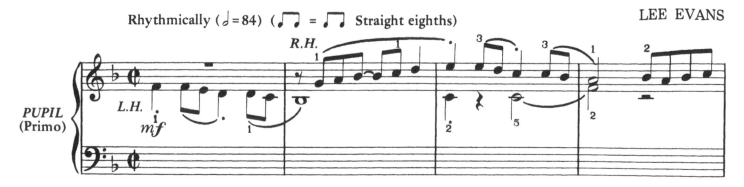

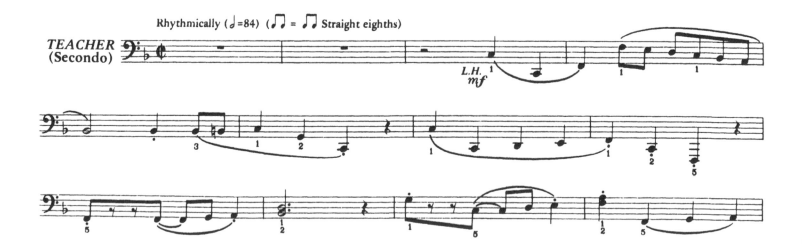

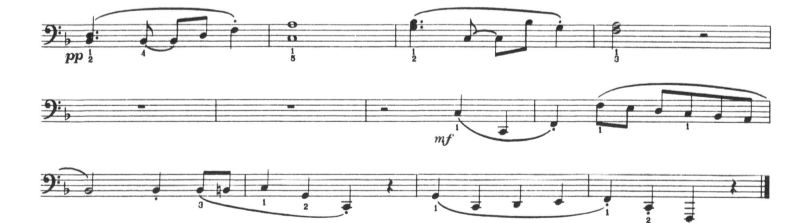

Blues Stomp

LEE EVANS

Latin From Manhattan

LEE EVANS

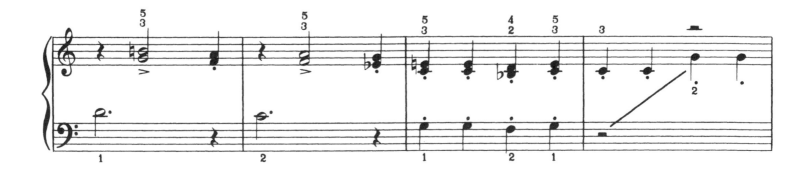

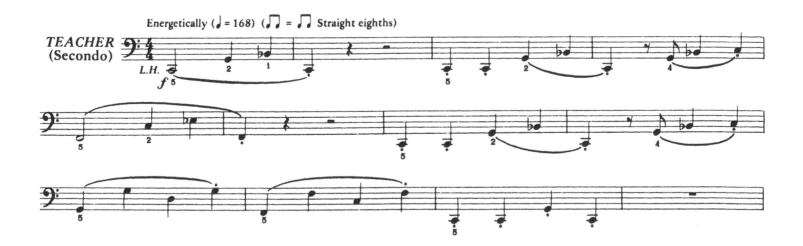

Gee Whiz!

LEE EVANS

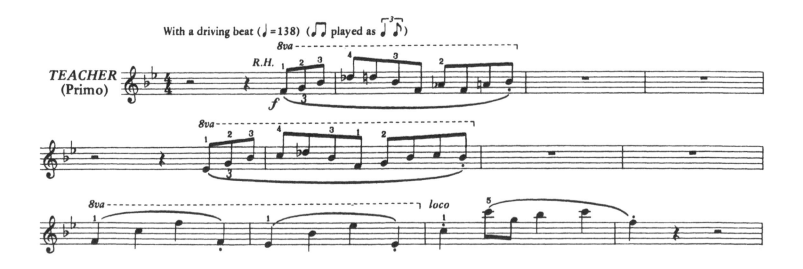

PP-3

Skateboard

LEE EVANS

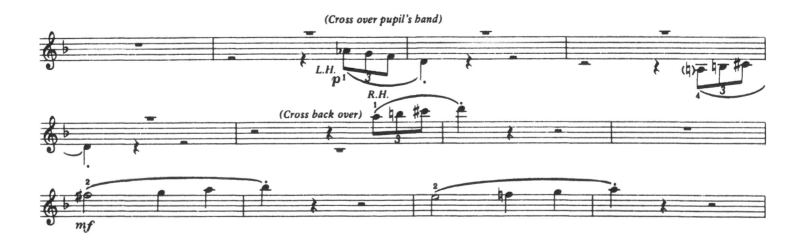

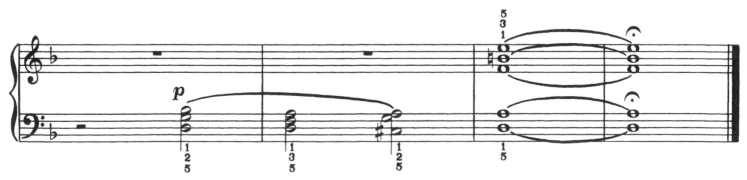